B

Illustrations © 2011 Sophia Janowitz

Design by Alex Miles Younger

The Domino Project

Published by Do You Zoom, Inc.

The Domino Project is powered by Amazon. Sign up for updates and free stuff at www.thedominoproject.com.

Kay, Sarah, 1988—

B / Sarah Kay

p. cm.

ISBN 978-1-612182-79-7

Printed in the United States of America

B

By Sarah Kay

Illustrated by Sophia Janowitz

THE
DOMINO
PROJECT
POWERED BY amazon.com

If I should have a daughter,

instead of Mom, she's going to call me Point B.

Because that way she knows that no matter what happens, at least she can always find her way to me.

And I'm going to paint the solar systems
on the backs of her hands,
so she has to learn the entire universe before she can say,

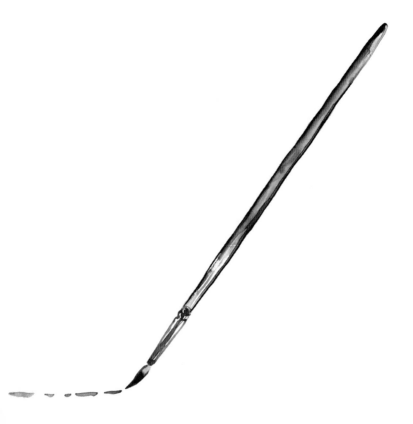

"Oh, I know that like the back of my hand."

And she's going to learn that this life will hit you
hard,
in the face;

wait for you to get back up,
just so it can kick you in the stomach,

but getting the wind knocked out of you is the only way
to remind your lungs how much they like the taste of air.

There is hurt here
that cannot be fixed
by Band-Aids or poetry.

So the first time she realizes that Wonder Woman
isn't coming, I'll make sure she knows
she doesn't have to wear the cape all by herself.

Because no matter how wide you stretch your fingers,
your hands will always be too small
to catch all the pain you want to heal.

Believe me, I've tried.

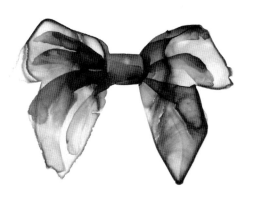

And Baby, I'll tell her, don't keep your nose
up in the air like that. I know that trick;
I've done it a million times.

You're just smelling for smoke
so you can follow the trail
back to a burning house,
so you can find the boy
who lost everything in the fire
to see if you can save him.

Or else—

find the boy
who lit the fire
in the first place,
to see if you
can change him.

But I know she will anyway.

So instead,
I'll always keep an extra supply of
chocolate and rain boots nearby,

      because there is no heartbreak that chocolate can't fix.

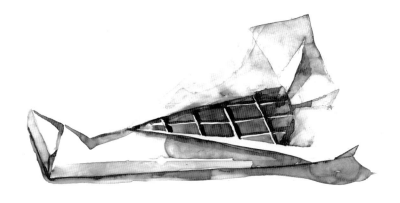

Okay, there's a few heartbreaks that chocolate can't fix. But *that's* what the rain boots are for.

Because rain will wash away everything, if you let it.

I want her to look at the world through
the underside of a glass-bottom boat,

to look through a microscope at the galaxies that exist
on the pinpoint of a human mind,

because that's the way my mom taught me—

That there'll be days like this.

There'll be days like this, my mama said.

When you open your hands to catch,
and wind up with only blisters and bruises;

when you step out of the phone booth and
try to fly, and the very people you want to
save are the ones standing on your cape;

when your boots will fill with rain,
and you'll be up to your knees in
disappointment.

And *those* are the very days you have
all the more reason to say thank you.

Because there's nothing more beautiful than the way
the ocean refuses to stop kissing the shoreline,
no matter how many times it's swept away.

You will put the wind in win(d)some,

                                    lose some.

You will put the star in starting over and over.

And no matter how many land mines erupt
in a minute, be sure your mind lands on
the beauty of this funny place called life.

And yes,

on a scale from one to over-trusting,

I am pretty damn naive.

But I want her to know that this world is made out of sugar: it can crumble so easily, but don't be afraid to stick your tongue out and taste it.

Baby,

I'll tell her,

remember your mama is a worrier,
and your papa is a warrior, and you
are the girl with small hands and big eyes
who never stops asking for more.

Remember that good things come in three's.

And so do bad things.

And always apologize when
you've done something wrong.
But don't you ever apologize
for the way your eyes refuse
to stop shining; your voice is small,
but don't ever stop singing.

And when they finally hand you heartache,
when they slip war and hatred under your door,
and offer you handouts on street-corners of
cynicism and defeat, you tell them that they

really ought to meet your mother.

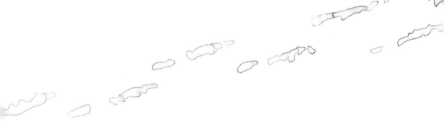

This poem was originally written for live performance. A video of Sarah performing this poem at the TED 2011 Conference in Long Beach, CA can be seen at: www.kaysarahsera.com

Acknowledgments

This book exists thanks to the magic and hard work of Sophia Janowitz, the patience and wisdom of Seth Godin and Alex Miles Younger, and the confidence and faith of Kelly Stoetzel, Chris Anderson, and the Scarecrow Brigade.

This poem exists thanks to the support and guidance of the NYC Urbana Poetry Slam, the Bowery Poetry Club, all the poets that light up the New York City poetry community, and mentors like Taylor Mali, Cristin O'Keefe Aptowicz, Jeanann Verlee, Anthony Veneziale, the Ferril-McCaffreys, and Rives.

These drawings exist thanks to the sight and insight of Joel Janowitz, Sarah Wainwright, Jan Kawamura-Kay, Jeffrey Kay, Deanne Urmy, Doug Fitch, Anne Lilly, Lily Herman, Michael Leibenluft, Katrina Landeta, Marianna Pease, and Rebecca, Marina, Mandy, and Terry Hopkins.

This joy exists thanks to the patience and love of family (you know who you are), friends who might as well be family (you know who you are), and especially Sophia Janowitz, James Schonzeit, Tatiana Gellein, Phil Kaye, Emily Borromeo, Kayla Ringelheim, Alex Kryger, and the Higher Keys.

This girl exists thanks to Mom, Pop, and PK.
        And Lion and Blankie.

About the Author and Illustrator:

Sarah Kay collects stories. Born and raised in New York City, Sarah began performing her poetry when she was fourteen years old. She made herself a home at the Bowery Poetry Club, where she was adopted by an unruly family of poets. In 2004, Sarah founded Project V.O.I.C.E. (Vocal Outreach Into Creative Expression) to encourage creative self-expression through Spoken Word Poetry. She has since performed and taught in venues and classrooms all over the world including the United Nations, where she was the featured poet for the launch of the *2004 World Youth Report*. In 2006, Sarah joined the NYC Urbana Poetry Slam team for the National Poetry Slam in Austin, Texas and was the youngest poet in the competition. That year, she was also featured on the sixth season of the television series *Russell Simmons presents HBO Def Poetry Jam*. In 2011, Sarah was a featured speaker at the TED Conference in Long Beach, California, where she performed her poem, "B." In between being a vagabond poet, Sarah can be found writing postcards, making documentary videos, and craving smoothies.

Sophia Janowitz spends most of her time making things. Over the past year, she has worked on a range of projects in theater, film, TV, stop-motion animation, and education. Most recently, she created props and sets with the production company Giants Are Small for *The Cunning Little Vixen* with the New York Philharmonic at Lincoln Center, and she helped build immersive sets for Punchdrunk's Off-Broadway production of *Sleep No More*. In 2010, Sophia collaborated on the shooting, editing, and writing of the feature-length film, *The Student Body*. Her illustrations have been featured in Yale University's *Manifesta* magazine and *The Yale Daily News*. Twice a day, Sophia can be found drawing people on the New York City subway.

Sarah and Sophia have been friends since they were three months old. Once, at age four, they were put in timeout for finger-painting all over the white wall of Sophia's bedroom. It was worth it.